M000007177

PRACTICAL CHANGE

Inspiration for Kicking Ass & Slaying Dragons...

By Noelle Federico

FIRST EDITION

© 2017 by Noelle Federico

All rights reserved. No part of this book may be reproduced without the permission in writing from the author, except by a reviewer who may quote brief passages in a review with appropriate credit; nor may any part of this book be reproduced, stored in a retrieval system, or transmitted in any form or by any means-electronic, photocopying, recording or other-without permission in writing from the publisher.

For information or permissions write:

One11 Publishing
872 S Milwaukee Ave, Ste 195
Libertyville, IL 60048

www.one11publishing.com
One11 Publishing is an imprint of
Newbern Consulting Group, LLC

Publisher: Sedrik Newbern

Cover Design by Creative Pearl www.creativepear.net
Dragon Illustration © Danilo Sanino | Dreamstime.com
Formatting by POP Color, Williston, VT
Back Cover photo by Tia Rooney Photography, Fairfax, VT

ISBN#   978-0-9982892-5-0

DEDICATION

To GOD who makes WAYS where there are no ways… always. For whatever I am and for whatever this will be to GOD goes all the glory…

To the little boy, now young man, that taught me how to be a Dragonslayer because I refused to fail him and I refused to let my dysfunction become his foundation. I may not be perfect kiddo and I know I can be a little hard to take, yet having you saved me from myself and forced me to slay dragon after dragon even when I didn't think I could… and now you are the reason that this work can contribute to so many… because being your mother forces me to fight and never give up. Antonio, YOU are my greatest gift. I love you MORE. XO

To my Working Single Mom followers, you inspire me every day to be better, do more and to keep GOING even when I would rather not.

THANK YOU…

In Fall of 2014, I drove from TN to VT to visit my family for Thanksgiving… at that time I had NO idea of the HUGE changes that were coming my way. At a restaurant in Concord, MA a Priest I had never seen before came up to me, introduced himself and said, "Noelle, remember this verse and everything will be ok." That verse has become my touchstone, I am sharing it with you:

"But they that
wait upon
the LORD shall
renew their strength;
they shall mount up
with wings as eagles;
they shall run,
and not be weary;
and they shall walk
and not faint."

~ Isaiah 40:31
King James Version

WITH GREAT GRATITUDE,
I ACKNOWLEDGE THESE PEOPLE...

My Mom and Steve, thank you for your love and support.

My Dad and Lin, thank you for always listening and cheering me on.

All four of my Grandparents, who watch from above...thank you for the foundation on which I stand.

My extended family, they have taught me much.

*My Prayer Warriors...Rodney, Lentini, Dave...*every morning, no matter what you guys are on the other end of the phone reminding me of WHO is really in control and reminding me that I will not fail. Thank you for all of the years behind us and all of the years ahead of us. You guys have my heart.

Mark... thank you for being my Guardian Angel, your presence in my life is a blessing beyond words.

Christine Bergeron... thank you for getting me through the last months... thank you for holding me up, believing in me, talking to me, yelling at me, forcing me to do what you knew I could...my life is blessed by you.

Keely Sullivan... my best friend since I was 12... you have seen me through decades and because of you I am a better person. I love you more than I can possibly say with mere words.

Karen, Stacey, Pam, Kim and Andy my forever companions, 30 years and counting... thank you especially for the support you have been these last months, for reminding me of who I was when I forgot and for reminding me never to settle for weak men or weak coffee. Thank you for every way you help me and for everything that you do for me...I truly, truly LOVE YOU ALL.

Debi... thank you for every way in which you bless my life.

Jeff...*thank you for all the ways that you helped me to become who I am now...my love and gratitude for always.*

Tracy & Christopher... *thank you for jumping on board to help with Boston and thank you for being my forever, prayer warrior friends.*

Jean, Selena, Paula and the rest of my VT crew... *thank you for your love, support and friendship...life is better now because of all of you.*

Q... *you are one of my favorite kids... I am thankful that you are Antonio's best friend and I know that your future holds amazing things and looking forward to being there to celebrate each and every one of them.*

Steve Philbrook *for showing me that chivalry is not dead, love you.*

Jane... *my sister from another mother, thank you for being in my life and for your love and support...you have my heart.*

IRISH...XOXO...Love you.

D. Gencarella, the original DRAGONSLAYER, *here's to the Biggest Dragon that we slayed together, I am thankful every day that you are still here reminding me how to keep fighting. I love you.*

Sedrik... *THANK YOU for agreeing to be part of this project and for being my friend for all these years, lets buckle-up buttercup and see what GOD will do with this...*

Miranda and Wayne from Soul Stone Wellness in St. Albans, VT... *thank you for your love and support and for helping me stay healthy and balanced.*

Michael Swaidner and the crew at POP Color in Williston, VT *for making everything I do look good:)*

Bryn & Associates... *the best legal team anyone in the world could ask for.*

Kim and Drew Hackett and Dirt Road Design *for everything they have been doing for me and with me for over a decade now. I love you both dearly and appreciate you more than words can convey.*

Bishop T.D. Jakes *for his work in the world, which inspires me year after year and ALWAYS seems to speak to me just when I need it the most...THANK YOU!*

Gary Vaynerchuk *for his work in the world which always makes me push harder. THANK YOU!*

Rusty *for our years of friendship, for your support during the last few months & always, for being AMAZING and BRILLIANT, love you xo*

To every other person that has been in my life these last 49 years, *whatever your role has been you have taught me something and I am grateful...*

"You gain strength, courage, and confidence by every experience in which you really stop to look fear in the face. You are able to say to yourself, 'I lived through this horror. I can take the next thing that comes along."

~ Eleanor Roosevelt

In regards to the book title and the #dragonslayer that will be used in association with this project, this is my working definition of 'DRAGON'...

DRAGON:

Any circumstance or situation that scares you, feels insurmountable, appears to be unchangeable or seems overwhelming.

Any person that frightens you or seems to have power over you.

Any seeming problem that appears to be bigger than you.

If it has you backed into a corner and you feel like you are going down... it's BULLSHIT!!!

Now is the time to pull everything you have within you together and FIGHT!

Pick up your sword and start fighting your way out, NO condition or circumstance has power over you.

It only seems that way if you allow it.

So STOP crying and feeling sorry for yourself. Life is hard. Period. So you be HARDER. Made of steel... nothing stops you, nothing gets in your way... and NOTHING backs you into a corner!

PICK UP YOUR SWORD and FIGHT!!!!

Out of you fighting and not giving up, solutions and opportunities will come. I know this. I have been in that corner many times and I know how to fight my way out. That's how I know you can do it too. I have been bankrupt, scared and nearly paralyzed by fear, yet here I sit. It did not kill me. It did not break me and I kicked the shit out of it.

So don't be afraid... instead BELIEVE in yourself the way that I believe in you and refuse to give in.

Fight... and when stuff knocks you down, get UP—TURN AROUND and SLAY SOME SHIT!

TABLE OF CONTENTS

INTRODUCTION

The first book in the Practical Change series was published in 2005... 12 years ago. HOLY COW! This second Practical Change volume has been a long time in the making...

I am now 49 years old and I have been the single mom of a son for going on 17 years now, I have never taken child support and his Father has never been an active person in his life. Solo parenting will press you and stretch you in ways that you never thought possible. It will push every button that you have, bring up every fear and every demon, it will scare you, enrich you, push you, slap you around, force you to be better and stronger than you ever thought possible and it will teach you to be a Dragonslayer... mostly because you have NO CHOICE and there is NO OTHER way out except through.

Parenting Antonio alone while starting, running and working for businesses proves to be an incredible training ground, I have lived through a bankruptcy, stupid romantic mistakes, betrayals, disappointments, heartbreaks as well as joys and celebrations. I have failed more times than I care to document, however I have NEVER, EVER given up... nor will I.

Many of you face challenges that you feel are insurmountable, you have days where you just want to give up or give in. Days where fear and darkness seem to get the better of you... THIS BOOK is for those days.

These pages contain things I have written to inspire you to kick ass and slay dragons on the days when you feel like you can't keep going. The book is designed so that you can open it anywhere and read something that will help you.

I have personally walked through all of the things that I talk about here and I continue to walk through them.

It is my intention that this book gives you a new way to look at your life and helps you to understand that you too are a FIERCE DRAGONSLAYER capable of incredible things.

Every day in every way things are getting better.

With Every Good Wish,

Noelle
Fairfax, VT
November 2017

WORDS OF WISDOM FROM PAPA FEDERICO...

Let's start this off with some sage advice from my Grandfather, a classic, old school Italian man... the hardest-working person I have ever met in my lifetime, he died 4 weeks before Antonio was born from two different kinds of cancer. He was Antonio T. Federico and my son was named for him as Antonio M. Federico.

I was raised in part by my grandparents and so when he became ill, frequently I was the one to drive him back and forth to the hospital and doctors appointments. After one such appointment we were called into the doctor's office, it was myself, Papa and my Uncle Mike. The doctor told us that Papa had colon and stomach cancer and started talking about treatments. At the time Papa was 82, he looked at the doctor and said, "Doc no offense but there will be no chemo, no radiation, and no treatment. It is what it is and I am going home."

The doctor said he had 6 months to live with no treatment, he lived a year...

After we left the hospital he wanted me to take him to his favorite bakery in Readville, MA on the way home. I was standing in the bakery, shell-shocked at the news I had just witnessed and he said, "Little girl (I was 31) don't be sad, I have had ONE HELL of a ride and when it's done, it's done." Papa taught us all how to live and he also taught us how to die, he left on his own terms, from his own house, his way and when he was damn good and ready. He only finished the 6th grade, he served this Country in the Navy and he was in the Local 4 Construction Union in Boston, MA for as long as I can recall.

He bought his house and then he worked 7 days a week straight until it was paid off, he went for a haircut every week and made his bed every, single damn day. He was a man of few words, however he was BIG on actions. He never really got to see what I have built, what I am still building, however he was my greatest teacher... he taught me how to KEEP GOING no matter what and I know he would be pleased that I am sharing some of his best advice with you ...

"Thanks to Papa we know how to get up every day even when we would rather not.

We know that no one else is going to do our work for us.

We know what's past is OVER and GONE.

We know that when we leave something it is for a reason and once we are done we don't go back... because the reason we left is still there...

We don't try to live in yesterday or get it back.

We keep GOING, NO MATTER WHAT.

We remember that disappointment is not the end of the world.

We know people will screw us over unwittingly, unconsciously or on purpose. We won't be stopped by it. We won't take it personal and we WILL keep a good eye on them after that...

We will also stay tuned to all the players... some people aren't wrapped too tight, some are living in another reality, some don't know their ass from a hole in the ground and others are just cruising through to see what they can get every day.

We remember that 75% of people have to be dealt with very carefully and some of them are dangerous characters... we remember to WATCH WHAT PEOPLE DO, not listen to what they say... actions speak volumes... promises are lip service unless followed up on with actions and results.

We do not count chickens before they are hatched.

We always have cash, just in case... "

***In 2015, God directed me back to New England after 11 years or so in TN. My Mother had encountered a health challenge and being an only child I felt that it was the right thing to do to head back. Antonio was about to enter High School and I bought a house in a town that I swore I would NEVER live in again. Turns out it has been a blessed decision, God always seems to know better than I do. I wrote this particular piece 24 days before I was to leave TN.

TENNESSEE THIS IS WHERE I LEAVE YOU

In 24 days, I will end an eleven year season in the state of Tennessee. As I was packing today I felt like I was walking through time, remembering all of the events of the last 11 years here. Ending a season is always bittersweet and I think it's good to recall the lessons learned within each season of your life. That being said, I thought I would document the lessons learned in Tennessee and share them with you.

Here we go... Lessons learned in the last decade:

• You CAN, in fact overcome ANY THING with prayer and a change in your thinking about the circumstance or situation... and I do mean ANY THING

• I am stronger than I thought

• I can survive betrayal of the worst degree and not be bitter

• I can forgive people without having to keep them in my life

• I can pray for people that have tried to harm me

• I can be alone and be happy

• Being alone is better than trying to turn myself into someone I don't know to stay with someone that I don't belong with

• GOD does, in fact, have everything under control

• GOD makes ways where there are no ways

• Trusting GOD will never, ever fail me

• Never get involved with someone that is not free to be involved, if someone is doing something else know you are worth enough to walk away until they finish it.

• Never start a relationship on the tail end of an old relationship

• Don't jump from one ending to a new beginning, take a space to heal, breathe and evaluate

🐾 PRACTICAL CHANGE

- Work hard and then work harder

- Be yourself no matter what

- Do not enable

- Do not over give

- Let people sit in their shit sometimes because that is the only way that they will learn

- Don't try to fix people, it won't work

- Watch ACTIONS, don't listen to words and when you see red flags in the actions, freaking PAY ATTENTION

- TRUST YOUR GUT

- TRUST YOUR FIRST REACTIONS to people, there is a warning there, HEED it

- If it doesn't feel right, it isn't—walk away

- Don't make excuses for dysfunctional shit just get away from it

- Be kind to people

- Stop complaining and realize that words matter—life and death in the power of your tongue—choose words wisely

- Don't settle

- I need to listen more sometimes and talk less

- Pay attention to people and think about how they will feel before you say or do something that effects them

- I am not easy to help

- Everything has a price

- My relationship with GOD is my most important one

- The people that really love you will never walk away from you, no matter what a shit you are

- BE GRATEFUL

Really, I grew up in Tennessee, I came here at 36 for work with no family and a 3 year old son… I was scared to death yet I knew that I needed to make my way as a single mom and the opportunity was one that I felt led to take. I can remember lying in bed on nights during that first year scared as hell wondering how it would all turn out. I had lived around my family my whole life and now I was here in a new place with nobody. I just kept praying and putting one foot in front of the other and I made a whole life here, made friends that became family and it all turned into an amazing season… there were some hard parts, even some terribly devastating parts… yet looking back over the 11 years—all in all it has been an amazing time of being blessed and being able to bless so many others. I came into my own here, in Boston (my hometown) we would say that I made my bones in Tennessee.

Now just like GOD called me here 11 years ago, He is now calling me back to New England and so back I go in 24 days to see what this new chapter will bring.

And so Tennessee this is where I leave you… thank you for keeping me safe, thank you for teaching me that I can do more than what I thought I could, thank you for all of the people that you sent into my life here, thank you for the memories and the lessons, for the people I have loved and for the people that taught me lessons, thank you for teaching me to trust GOD more, thank you for all of it, the good, the bad and the ugly parts… you have made me what I am now and for that I am so grateful… until we meet again…

"Hardships
often prepare
ordinary people
for extraordinary
destiny."

~ C.S. Lewis

WHEN GOD SHUTS A DOOR...

When God closes a door stop banging on it... meaning He closed it for a reason. We may not understand or agree with God's reasons and timing; however we need to trust them. God has the bigger plan and He knows what we need better than we do.

Having Faith means trusting what we cannot yet see. Sometimes when we are seeking the answer to something we need to let go of it and simply do the tasks before us. Trust that when the time is right the way will be made unmistakably clear to us. At times this can look like stepping out where there seems to be no road under our feet; there are times when we have to follow God's prompts to go forward even when we do not see the pavement in front of us. During these times God acts as our eyes, He sees the road ahead and He directs the path on which we walk, put one foot in front of the other... do the tasks that are before you each day and just keep putting one foot in front of the other.

We may not see the whole road, yet as we step each time there is solid ground that appears beneath our feet. God makes a way where there is no way, some days this is my mantra...

So when God shuts a door just leave it closed and go find the open one...

TAKE TIME TO LISTEN...

Webster's defines listen as "to give ear to, to hear, to pay attention to, to give something consideration."

How many of us are actively listening to people, to GOD? Or are we soooo busy with our own agendas and our electronic devices that we have forgotten the fine art of LISTENING?? Many things can happen in the silence of us listening, we can hear God's will for us, we can hear people's ideas, concerns and needs... we can be thoughtful while we are actively giving attention to someone else.

Attention is life-giving and listening to someone IS giving them your undivided attention, that means no cell phone, no iPhone, no iPad, no computer —just you paying attention to them and listening to HEAR what they are really saying.

Lots of times we "listen" and we don't "hear"—we automatically think we know what the other person is saying so we tune them out before they even get to finish speaking. In sales a good listener does very well, in life a good listener also does very well. People thrive from your attention and everyone wants to be "heard".

Take quiet time to listen to GOD, to listen for His direction and timing for us—so many times we try to push things in our timing when if we just waited for God's timing the path would have been so much smoother.

Take a moment and listen to someone today, put everything aside and really listen. You will be glad you did.

LEAVE CRAZY TO THE CRAZIES

It's funny really when you find yourself reacting to someone else's childish and foolish behavior... you know what they are trying to do... get your attention... they can't get your attention like an adult, by actually conversing... so they start acting out... because of course, any attention for these types of dysfunctional people is a win.

So they act out and you find yourself, much to your horror, reacting to them. Instead of doing what needs to be done and ignoring them. People like this DO NOT deserve our attention, their communication skills are sub-par and instead of having effective communication that works they fall into passive-aggressive, narcissistic behavior patterns. People like this are flawed at such a deep level that they don't even see that they are like hamsters running on a wheel to nowhere.....FAST.

Insanity is doing the same thing over and over again and expecting a different result. So us thinking that these people will behave differently is just as pitiful as what they are doing in the first place. When people SHOW you who they are, BELIEVE them.

Leave the crazy to the crazy people, grab your toys and exit the building... do not react to people like this—respond to them by ignoring their attempts to engage you and move on. People like this will only steal your energy and keep you from doing what you need to do... if someone wants to be in your life, let them ask. If you need to chase they don't deserve to be on your radar.

You are worth so much more than that. The people that belong with you will make themselves known and it won't be a circus, it will be peaceful. So stop reacting and everything else will take care of itself.

PRACTICAL CHANGE

"HELL is wanting
to be somewhere
other than
WHERE YOU ARE."

~ Stephen Levine

RANGER UP...

What you have right now is a product of what you have spent your attention on in the past. Whatever you give your attention to and whatever you speak is what you will manifest. Don't be fooled into thinking that what you watch, read and talk about doesn't matter— IT DOES. Your life will manifest itself as you lay it out in your thinking, speaking and acting.

If you don't like what you see in front of you start changing your actions... you can't expect to sit around and beg God to change your life when you are polluting your mind with crap and sitting around waiting for money to fall out of the sky... get up off your ass and make a change... read some affirmations, get to the gym, take a walk, help someone else, stop whining and complaining that life isn't working out the way you wanted it to. YOU are responsible for what happens in your life, not your parents, not the government, not your ex.....YOU!

Nobody is going to solve your issues except you... this is the cold, hard truth and it is also the key to setting you free from what is stopping you in your life. GOD is WAITING for YOU to DO SOMETHING!!!!! So get moving... RANGER UP, quit complaining and start being part of the solution. Now GO!

"When you recognize that you will thrive not in spite of your losses and sorrows, but because of them, that you would not have chosen the things that happened in your life, but you are grateful for them, that you will hold the empty bowls eternally in your hands, but you also have the capacity to fill them?

THE WORD FOR THAT IS HEALING."

~ Cheryl Strayed

***Special thanks to Crystal Rose-Coats for sending me this quote.

ONE BLUEBERRY AT A TIME...

An addiction is when you continue to let things damage you even though you know the destructive nature of what you are doing... Insanity is doing the same thing over and over again and expecting a different result. Insane behavior supports an addiction or addictive behavior because it helps you tell yourself that things will turn out differently this time, it helps you mask the obvious and live in the hope that 'this' is different than the time before. Insane behavior is just that– INSANE. If you are stuck in a pattern or a circumstance that isn't changing, as long as you STAY STUCK THERE it WILL NOT CHANGE. You will see the same wheel turn round and round and you will keep telling yourself that the result will be different... it won't.

In order to change the turn of the wheel we need to change ourselves and our circumstances. We lose hope when we feel like we have lost the power to enact change, the truth is we never lose the power to enact change... the God-part of our nature is always lying there waiting to be called upon... if we give power to that and ask God for help we can enact whatever changes we wish. Consequently, if we give power to the darker sides of our nature we will continue down the road of insane behavior.

There is never a convenient time to push ourselves to give up a behavior that no longer serves us; these behaviors wear all kinds of names: drug addiction, alcohol addiction, food addictions, being overweight, staying in relationships that have long been over, guilt, gambling, sex addictions, over-spending, involving ourselves in relationships with unavailable people, etc etc. Whatever costume your behavior wears it is stealing your aliveness and it has you in such a state of reactivity that you cannot even see your REAL life because all you are doing is riding the crazy train.

Some of us have been riding for so long now that we actually think we are making progress... REALITY CHECK- you only make progress when you get OFF the train and realize that you have been riding on it, at this point you get to choose a different course. A fish that lives in a fishbowl has no idea that he lives in there as all he knows is the limited conditions of the bowl. A human being stuck in a behavior shares the same limited understanding of their life, they think what they are living in is all there is…

Enacting change starts with recognizing that we have something that needs to be changed, the 12 step programs call it admitting that we have a problem and that works too. Use whatever method or program you need to use to recognize the behavior that doesn't work. The important thing is to recognize it because of course you cannot change something that you cannot even SEE.

Making major behavioral shifts is like picking up blueberries that have fallen on the floor. If you have ever dropped a container of blueberries on the floor you will fully appreciate this comparison.

When you drop a container of blueberries they roll EVERYWHERE… first you swear and become angry that you were stupid enough to drop the container in the first place and then you quickly resolve yourself to the fact that you have to pick them up. You can't pick them up in handfuls because you will crush them, so you have to pick them up one by one and as you do that some of them roll away under things and you have to peer under there and roll them out. The blueberries also NEVER fit back into the container the way that they were before you dropped them, so you have to artfully maneuver them back into the container to try and get it to close again. When you are picking up the blueberries they sometimes fall out of your hands again and you end up grabbing the same blueberry several times… all in all, a tedious process that causes one to gasp in horror when a container is dropped…

A shift in behavior is like this as it is one small change at a time and sometimes you drop another blueberry and you have to pick it up again and again. You can't scoop all the blueberries back into the container at once or you will crush them, you can't change a behavior in a day or it won't stick. REAL change, REAL behavioral shifts come over time, in stages, one blueberry at a time and eventually you have them all and you can reclose the container. Eventually your small changes become a big shift and one day along the way you wake up and realize that you are free from your insanity and that you have clarity you never had before. Important to remember that when you drop a blueberry in the 'picking up' process all is not lost, just reach down and pick it up again. When you are making changes and you go back and repeat a behavior that doesn't work, it's okay… just remember that you are shifting and next time make a different choice… change can be embodied one blueberry at a time…

SEE A BRIDGE FOR WHAT IT IS...

Webster's defines bridge for my purposes here as "a thing that provides connection, contact or transition". Sometimes Life provides us a bridge that we mistake as 'the solution'... there are times when we need help, yet we are not truly ready for what's next and in those times Life provides a bridge that transitions us from who we are to who we must become. Often in this process we mistake the 'bridge' as the solution.

There are times in our lives when moving to the next, higher stage of being is required and often we are so caught up in the circumstances of the moment that we can't see our way clear to make the changes on our own. It is at these times that Life sends us a bridge to help us transition from who we are to who we must become... the bridge can look like a new situation, a new friend, a mentor, a boss, a relationship interest, a new job opportunity, a move from one place to another, a new work project... whatever way we need to have it in order for it to be effective, that is the way Life will send it.

When the desired transition is complete the bridge is no longer needed and often the loss of the bridge is mistaken as a hurtful experience, when in fact it is a blessing because it means we have transitioned and are ready for the next level which is a better place for us.

There is a teaching that says "the blessing comes before the challenge"—meaning that we create a gift for ourselves and then we must create a challenge to overcome so that we can readily receive it... in that same way we create a bridge to help us become who and what we need to be.

Understand that a bridge is a gift, just because something is utilized to get you from point A to point B doesn't make it any less meaningful or worthy—it just means that a bridge isn't forever, it is a situation that is meant to last only for a certain period of time whether it is one week or 5 years. A bridge isn't meant to build a life on; it is meant to cross you from one place to the other.

Think of all of the things that haven't worked out the way we thought they would or should have... reframe them as bridges, every, single one of them.

To see something as a bridge allows you to forgive yourself or someone else for what you previously may have labeled "failure". To see a completed situation as a 'bridge' allows you to reconstruct the past in your mind and out of that you have the ability to create a different future. Imagine if you had an attitude of gratitude about your 'bridges' instead of a story of how horrible they all were... imagine turning a string of previously labeled 'failures' into a path of bridges that are taking you just where you need to go... there is a lot of freedom in that and a lot of power.

"When you want
something,
all the universe
conspires in
helping you
to achieve it."

~ Paulo Coelho

***Special thanks to Bernae Rogers for this one

PRACTICE GENEROSITY

Learn to practice generosity like a habit. St. John of the Cross says that "a generous heart will never go part way". Let's talk about what true generosity is... understanding generosity as a principle will help you realize that it isn't just about buying things, it is about so much more than that...

When you practice generosity you understand that there is an endless supply of everything that is required and that if you give some of 'yours' away it will be given back to you. No lack was ever created by giving, poverty never stems from generosity. Anne Frank said, "No one has ever become poor by giving."

Poverty and lack are stimulated by a belief that there is a limited supply and this belief helps people to be selfish and hold on to what is 'theirs'. GOD bestowed upon us an unending supply of substance which is manifested by the spirit of generosity.

What if everything you 'had' wasn't really yours anyway, what if God gave it to you so that you could be generous with it and when you did that He would give you more? If you understood that as a truth how much would it change the way you act in your daily life? If someone asked you for a ride or for five dollars and you knew that if you gave it to them then God would see it multiplied back to you... would you then be more willing to give it?

Practicing generosity requires us to understand that we have been blessed with ABUNDANT supply, available to us by simply asking the Divine to send it and then having certainty that it will come.

As I said, nobody ever became poor from giving; people have become poor by living in fear that there is a limited supply of money, work, good etc. When our willingness to give dries up from fear then we actually BLOCK our Divine Supply from being able to reach us. Generosity and the practice of it help to keep the Divine pipeline moving in a positive direction. Be generous today with whatever you have to give... time, attention, money, actions... A generous heart is a happy heart.

🐾 PRACTICAL CHANGE

LEAVE YOUR CRITICAL SELF BEHIND...

Joel Osteen says, "If you don't have something good to say... ZIP IT!" and that is good advice because have you noticed how critical we have become? It seems like we are always complaining about something and finding fault with something else... complaining, judging, evaluating and finding fault have become as commonplace as brushing our teeth. It starts first thing in the morning... the coffee line is too long, our kids are too slow, there is too much traffic, the news is all bad, people can't drive, the weather isn't right, etc., etc...

Consider how much energy we expend on complaining and being critical. Imagine what could happen if we turned that into a positive experience; imagine if we actually looked for the good in situations; called attention to it; acted upon it. There is good in everything but we often need to look hard to find it and sometimes we just have to trust that it is present whether we see it or not. Faith is a very powerful tool that can be used to alter even the worst of circumstances. However, like any tool it must be used often in order for us to strengthen it.

Criticism can also be a powerful force for change if used in the correct fashion. There is destructive criticism and there is constructive criticism.

Destructive criticism points out what is wrong with situations and people with no solution—that man is a slob, that woman is unhealthy, that building is dirty...

Constructive criticism can be used as force to correct problems and unite people for the greater good because it offers an action at the end of the complaint... that outfit doesn't suit you, however I have one that does... there is trash everywhere so let's pick it up... you are always late so let me buy you a new watch...

The most bothersome issue is that people fail to recognize that constant destructive criticism kills joy, good humor and hope... it causes people to despair and feel like life is just too much trouble. It can create a terrible momentum that becomes almost impossible for the target of criticism to overcome.

Think about the people in your life that are always finding fault with someone or something. How enlivening is it to be in their presence for more than 5 minutes??? The air can literally seem to become thick and foul. You may even feel as if a shadow descends upon you the longer you stay in their presence.

Criticism and cynicism shut life down instantaneously... possibility cannot exist where there is no listening for it and critical/cynical people have no field of vision for what is good or what is possible.

Critical/cynical people look through a particular filter that only allows them to see more of what they talk about and since they always talk about what doesn't work or what is wrong, that is all they are able to see. Their blindness to the positive possibilities that abound is not only dangerous to those within their circle of influence, it is contagious!

Most of them don't even notice what limited vision they have given themselves. They just go around believing that life sucks, people are awful, and that misery is the default setting that they must endure.

Stuck in this way of looking they will not even see a random act of kindness or goodwill... they will only continue to gather evidence that life is hard and people will hurt you.

Life is truly what you make it and we have the choice in every, single moment to interpret circumstances as good or bad. We can call to the possibility in something or we can be defeated and harmed by it, the choice is always ours.

It takes a particular kind of person to see the good and call to the positive aspects in a situation... a person like this has the ability to transform any circumstance into something beneficial. That particular kind of person is in ALL of us – we simply have to let that inner optimist emerge.

You have the power to be a person like this… it takes courage, faith and strength of character and it takes the understanding that life is far more contributed to by the ongoing choice for good. The first step to a positive approach is to simply take that first step with an attitude of opportunity and confidence that what happens next in life is something to embrace rather than fear.

"Do What You Can With All You Have, Wherever You Are."

~ Theodore Roosevelt

***Special thanks to Jessica Neal for this one

SOMETIMES YOU JUST GOTTA MAKE IT UP...

Joy or no joy, happy or unhappy... that choice is yours and yours alone. Contrary to what you believe, things and people and circumstances can't make you 'happy' or 'unhappy', only YOU can do that.

Granted being happy for no reason or being joyful no matter what takes skill and determination, however it CAN be accomplished. You can be happy and joyful no matter what, whether you are shoveling crap out of the cat's litter box or dancing at a ball with a gorgeous partner... the choice is yours and yours alone.

To be happy and joyful no matter what requires you to develop the skill of making something up out of nothing, generating pure unabashed enthusiasm for no reason what-so-ever. This CAN be done and I know this because I was trained to do it... when I was about 14 or 15 I wanted to go to the mall with my friends and my Mom wanted me to first help her wrap some presents. Being a cooperative teenager (NOT) I did not wish to wrap the presents first, I wanted to go to the mall...

My Mom said that if I could wrap the presents with her displaying an attitude of joy and enthusiasm, I could then go to the mall, mind you now the wrapping of the actual presents could have taken about 30 minutes if I had been more willing... instead it took all night...

I said that I would wrap the presents, however I was angry and sullen and if you know my Mom that was just plain unacceptable... we had a swinging door from our kitchen into her office and she said "go into the kitchen and come back through that door with enthusiasm".... .so the sullen, angry teenager went through the door stomping her feet and came back through with some pathetic version of "happy" to wrap gifts... .Mom said, "NO PASS" —do it again.

Keep in mind now my Mom is a Prosperity Teacher and a Results Coach so my whole life was a classroom and this incident was no different... back I went madder than ever through the damn door... back again I came, madder… "NO PASS, do it again"…

Back I went, complaining that I WASN'T happy, so how could I generate 'happiness and enthusiasm', my Mom "just MAKE IT UP, do it again"…

Back I came crying about how MEAN she was and how none of my friends mothers did this crazy stuff, blah, blah, blah… ."NO PASS, do it again"

This went on for several hours, back and forth through that silly, damn door and then FINALLY… I got it… I had to just CHOOSE IT, I had to MAKE IT UP OUT OF NOTHING. Was there a "reason" to be happy? NO! Was there evidence to support my enthusiasm??? NO! Did that matter??? NO!

I just had to generate something out of nothing to get the damn job done and in that moment I mastered it, I got it and I came flying through that door the happiest son of a gun you ever saw! Mom said "PASS!!!!!"

That was one of the defining moments of my life and one of my greatest lessons, my Mother knew what she was doing, she still does… she was and continues to train me for excellence, she trained me that day that it doesn't matter what is happening all around you, you CAN CHOOSE to be joyful, happy and enthusiastic no matter what. That choice is yours and you simply make it up. You can do this whether you are sitting in traffic, waiting tables, cleaning toilets, parenting kids or sitting in the sun on a tropical island.

Life brings to you what you bring to it, if you bring complaining and despair then life will bring you more of that… if you bring happiness and enthusiasm then life will multiply that for you.
So today… .run through that swinging door with CRAZY JOY AND ENTHUSIASM just because you can… I dare you!

"The most beautiful people
I've known are those
who have known trials,
have known struggles,
have known loss,
and have found their
way out of the depths."

~ Elisabeth Kubler-Ross

FINDING THE COURAGE TO SAY GOODBYE...

It takes an immense amount of courage to say good-bye to something that isn't excellent. So many of us put up with circumstances, conditions and relationships that are not really working and there truly IS a time when it is appropriate to say good-bye so that healing can happen and new good can occur.

Yes, there is a time to stand up and fight for something, a time to make changes, a time to try new behaviors... all of that... however when enough time has passed and you feel that you have done all you can and you are still not seeing the result you require, it may just be time to say "good-bye".

Saying good-bye to something isn't "bad", it isn't "giving up", it is having the wisdom to see that beating a dead horse is a fool hardy exercise... you exhaust yourself and the horse is still dead.

When you say good-bye you can do it with love, that is possible... you can do it with acknowledgement of contributions made, you can release and set something free with great gratitude and love and forgiveness for those things that didn't turn out the way you wanted them to.

Granted most people say good-bye in anger or fear or guilt or some combination of those... it doesn't need to be like that. Endings are also new beginnings where new blessings can show up, where new good can appear.

When you prune a tree it seems like a terrible thing, you cut living branches from it and it looks terrible for a while... then it starts to grow and fill out stronger than it ever was before... new life comes to it when before it looked almost dead and barren. Good-bye can be like that, it feels awful, it looks awful... times goes by and then new LIFE comes zooming in bringing with it new blessings we couldn't see before.

So many people hang on to things that have been unworkable for so

PRACTICAL CHANGE

long… jobs, relationships, items, marriages etc… they hang on because they are scared to death to let go… letting GO is letting GOD… it is trusting something greater than yourself to take care of you and it is knowing that with every ending comes a new start for something not yet seen.

When appropriate have the courage to say good-bye, everything that you want could very well be on the other side of good-bye….

"You never know
how Strong
you are,
until Strong
is the ONLY
choice you have..."

~ Bob Marley

***Special thanks to Jessica Langhofer-Cabrales for this one

WARRIOR... aka.
DRAGONSLAYER MENTALITY...

Be a Warrior—ok, great so what does that mean? It means doing the things that you don't 'want' to do with enthusiasm, it means saying yes to something when it is more comfortable to say no, it means getting out of bed and running at your day full speed ahead, singing at the top of your lungs and knowing that you will prevail over circumstances.

Warriors don't give up, they don't give in, they don't do what is popular—they stand their ground, they make noise and you know when one has come into the room. True Warriors are a force of nature and we don't shy away from what is hard or uncomfortable... we wear the Armor of GOD and it is our job to demonstrate LOVE in action as well as demonstrate how to WORK with no story and no excuses. Warriors execute results and while other people are busy whining about circumstances and complaining about the economy, we, the WARRIORS are busy getting things done and making things work.

Right now there is a crazy story in the news every day that tells us of some event that is horrible... for those of us that are awake it is our job to pray for the people in those situations and then turn attention to what is GOOD and what is RIGHT and shine a light on where the JOY is—it is also our job to clothe ourselves in the Armor of the Most High and get BUSY doing HIS work—blessing things, helping people that are afraid, giving till it hurts, making other people have better days and trusting that there IS a Divine plan and the more we are Warriors for that the better off everything is.

Today... be a WARRIOR and declare to anything that isn't working ... " I WILL NOT YIELD"—once you draw that line every horrid circumstance will crumble into a blessing, mind you that line is hard to hold... refusing to yield means doing so NO MATTER WHAT IT LOOKS LIKE in any given moment. So don your Armor and draw your line in the sand against what isn't working... and think WARRIOR!

"This is the true joy in life,
the being used for a purpose recognized
by yourself as a mighty one;
the being a force of nature
instead of a feverish,
selfish little clod of ailments and grievances
complaining that the world will not devote
itself to making you happy.

I am of the opinion that my life belongs to
the whole community, and as long as I live it is
my privilege to do for it whatever I can.

I want to be thoroughly used up when
I die, for the harder I work the more
I live. I rejoice in life for its own sake.
Life is no "brief candle" for me.
It is a sort of splendid torch
which I have got hold of for the moment,
and I want to make it burn as brightly
as possible before handing it
on to future generations."

~ George Bernard Shaw

PRACTICAL CHANGE

LEAVE A LEGACY

Gurdjieff ([1877-1949], priest, physician, teacher, author of 'Meetings With Remarkable Men') tells us that to live in a truly creative and dynamic way; we would have to think in a completely new way. He encourages that to be completely fulfilled, we must engage in our own conscious evolution. In his work he also speaks about conscious labor and intentional suffering and about the importance of undertaking the burden of responsibility for serving the future... in other words building a legacy...

Gurdjieff's student J.G. Bennett "... adopted as a major theme of his life and work the teaching known as "The Fourth Way". This is very simply that in the face of a threat, whether environmental disaster, war and conquest, or economic collapse, those persons who are able to do so must accept the responsibility of guiding and supporting the less resourceful, but not through the conventional institutions of government or religion, but rather on the level of new ideas and attitudes, inspiration and spiritual regeneration. As many Sufi teachers have done, he hinted at a world of experience in which the laws are quite other than those governing the material world – in some cases, the reverse. Those who are able to decipher this riddle must inevitably dedicate themselves to serving humanity, and the future of our world." (www.jgbennett.net)

Those of us that understand that there is far more to life than what we can physically "see", understand also that we have a responsibility to encourage other people not to be limited by their own thinking. I speak often of the fact that you should never, ever judge or evaluate a situation by the way that it looks in any given moment — you should only ever operate from your intention about what the outcome will be. So many people are stopped in their tracks because they think that the obstacles they encounter are "real"... they fail to understand that what makes obstacles "real" is believing that they exist. There are people that are never stopped, people that never quit... if one way gets blocked up they find another... these are the people that succeed and know how to live 'outside the box'... these are the kind of people you want to know.

I mostly live in a conversation called 'what's next… what else needs doing', the past few weeks I have been living in a question called, "What is your Legacy?"

It is interesting that when you begin to engage in this discussion, your life and what you have done or not done shows up in a whole different light… complaints and grievances don't hold much water in the Legacy conversation… 25 years after you're dead nobody is going to care that your back hurt or you had a cold or a headache or that you were too tired to do the laundry. Some people have told me that their children are their legacy and that is certainly true for all of us that are parents, however, for me that isn't enough.

I want to leave something that breathes on long after I checked out… something that is dedicated to making people's lives better, something that educates people and teaches them how to succeed… something that helps those that need helping… something that can be carried forward … something that makes a difference…

My life will change from living in the question, "What is your Legacy?"… do me a favor and take a moment to answer that question for yourself… honestly. How are you giving back, who are you helping, and what are you serving besides yourself? How do you serve the future?

I have a theory that if people lived in these questions life would take on a whole new meaning… if people lived for a purpose bigger than themselves the small annoyances they suffer would become much less significant.

Certainly not the average conversation, but average conversations never create much growth or much action—they also don't cause you to think much.

PRACTICAL CHANGE

POSSIBILITY EXISTS...

A statement on my office wall reminds me—always– that you can accept the reality of a situation, however you are NEVER to accept its permanence... Possibility is NEVER absent. How many people even really understand what this means?

It means that– yes, SHIT happens... however when it is happening it is not set in stone, when something doesn't go your way or turn out the way you want, it doesn't mean that your life sucks! It SIMPLY means that the particular relationship or situation did not turn out the way you wanted. Possibility is NEVER absent; it is only hidden from our view when our negative thoughts and words obstruct it. We are the only people that can keep our own good from us... not your boss, your spouse, your kids or the government... only YOU. You keep your good from coming to you by engaging in thoughts that are not useful... thoughts like :

"I will never have another girlfriend like THAT"

" I will never have money again"

"My career is awful"

"The economy is bad, it's no use"

"I'm this old and this is what my life is like??? REALLY??"

"My car is old, my living quarters are awful"

"Everyone around me is annoying"

And ON and ON and ON it goes... if you let it. Once that dark ball gets rolling in your mind, it's hard to stop. It takes a GREAT amount of effort to stay positive in the face of anything, a GREAT amount of effort to stay in faith that things will be better, a GREAT amount of effort to trust that good is coming. Nothing good comes easily, nothing lasting is formed without great effort. Life is not supposed to be easy, that Staples button is a crock of shit... the fantasy of that button manifested itself from a society that is becoming lazier by the day... HARD WORK is how you gain anything that matters and you know why you get to keep it after you worked your butt off for it? Because you EARNED it... you did whatever you needed to do to get it and you elevated yourself in the process and so now you earned something and you became a different person because of that.

Whining and wishing for the EASY button will bring you a whole lot of NOTHING and if you do manage to grab something from the EASY track, you won't be able to keep it because spiritually you didn't earn it, nor did you change in order to receive it. Why do you think that so many people that win the lottery end up losing it and having their lives ruined? Because they didn't EARN it.

Your life is the way it is because that is how your life is supposed to be at this moment, you are where you are because you need to learn something, because you have to grow and test new skills... if everything was EASY you wouldn't learn a damn thing.

There is GOOD in every situation even when you can't SEE it! It is there... it will show itself faster if you can remain open to the fact that possibility is never absent, possibility is like GOD... ever present...

I am not saying that you should avoid whatever 'reality' you are currently in, I am saying be mindful that it is simply a PASSING circumstance... DO NOT accept the permanence of any situation... EVER

Everything can be altered... everything...

🐾 PRACTICAL CHANGE

"Owning our story and loving ourselves through that process is the bravest thing we will ever do."

~ Brene Brown

***Special thanks to Emily Smith-Conlon for this one

COMPLACENCY vs. CHANGE

It is difficult to initiate change when one becomes complacent. Webster's defines complacent as marked by self-satisfaction especially when accompanied by unawareness of actual dangers or deficiencies. The key in this definition is the part about being unaware of 'actual dangers or deficiencies'... complacent is a place in consciousness where nothing new happens, it is an area of 'no change occurring'... when change is not occurring things become stale and stagnant.

Becoming complacent is like settling for what you got instead of being uncomfortable and moving on to get what you WANT. People do this in business, they do it in relationships, they do it in marriages and they do it with their health. CHANGE is hard work, it is uncomfortable, it doesn't plateau... it keeps things moving... when things are moving new growth happens.

Complacency is dangerous because it allows for you to stay in situations and circumstances that don't work... we all do that, we make excuses for people and things, we tell ourselves it is ok even when we see and hear 'RED FLAGS'... when we do that, when we stay in things that don't work to their best ability, we steal a little bit of our aliveness every day, every day that we make concessions and excuses is a day that we lose a little bit of ourselves.

It is upsetting to make changes, life is messy... out of mess comes order... out of chaos new things are formed.

"Success is
walking from
failure to failure
with no loss
of enthusiasm."

~Winston Churchill

SOME BLESSINGS WEAR
A HELL OF A DISGUISE...

On my office wall filled with quotes—I see one that sparks a flash of inspiration... it is an anonymous quote that reads, "Some blessings wear a hell of a disguise... " Well, well, well... now yes they do!

My faith in God has taught me that there is good in everything even when it can't be seen. I am of the opinion that you have to trust that even in your darkest hour the good is there and eventually it will come to bless and benefit you. All of this is easier said than done. There have been quite a few times when life has whipped me around to the almost breaking point and in those hours it took all my courage to trust that good was there somewhere. Days, years, months later I could see the blessing... however in those moments I didn't see squat!

Several people in my life right now are living in those dark moments, one is losing her house from bankruptcy and another is struggling with a stinging betrayal. It is hard to counsel them that there is good somewhere present in the current circumstances. I know for them that it is there, however it is hard for them to stay steady now and trust that for themselves.

When our blessings are wearing a hell of a disguise and it seems as if life is against us, the most important thing that we can do is to know that good is present somewhere, somehow... it is vital in the middle of urgent circumstances to keep your head clear and above water... it is imperative to react to things according to the outcome that you want to see— not according to the way it looks at any given moment. Remember that the miracle doesn't come unless there is complete certainty and trust on your part. From what I have read, according to a Hebrew version of the Bible, when Moses created the miracle of the parting of the Red Sea, he and his followers had to walk into the sea knowing that it would part for them... from what is written, the sea did not part until they were in the water up to their nostrils—only then did the sea become dry land. They had to walk into the sea with the CERTAINTY that it would part for them. As they were walking further and further in, there were moments that it looked like they were going to drown... they kept going because they trusted and they were certain that the sea would make way for them... IT DID!

We must use this lesson in our own lives, every day. You must be certain that life will make way for you to have the outcome that you desire, provided that it is for the highest good of everyone involved. Understand that the highest good in a situation is not always what our ego desires. Some of us try to push 'our will' instead of Divine Will... that doesn't usually work out so well.

When your intentions and desires are pure, life will move heaven and earth to assist you. Blessings are usually disguised to help us acquire qualities that we may not learn otherwise... hence the old saying "if God brings us to it... God will bring us through it"... this is good news, it means we never get anything we can't handle.

So the next time life is kicking your butt remember that there is good in there somewhere... even if you can't see it, trust that it is present. The willingness to trust for the possibility of good has the power to shift your state of mind and therefore the entire situation.

EVERYTHING FOR A REASON

I am a firm believer in the statement 'everything happens for a reason' and I look at every uncomfortable situation in my life and try to see what it wants to teach me. Sometimes I see the lesson right away and sometimes I just have to trust that it's there and that I will see it eventually. I have learned some of my most valuable lessons from the people and situations that have distressed me the most. When you are open to the possibility of being contributed to by every event in your life the unpleasant events seem to go by faster.

I have also learned that one of the best ways to diffuse an attack is to apologize for something right in the middle of it. For instance, "I'm sorry that you feel I've insulted you", or "I'm sorry that you think I hurt you on purpose". People attack you because they want attention or they are unhappy with themselves. If someone attacks you in conversation and you do not respond or you apologize this will diffuse the situation. A person can only fight with you if you let them. You cannot argue with someone who refuses to be engaged by you.

I have been told that what we don't like about other people represents something that we don't like about ourselves. If this is true the first action would be to forgive ourselves for all the things that we find unacceptable. If we can forgive ourselves successfully then we can move ahead to start forgiving others. Truly, truly everyone is going along doing the best that they can for who they are—maybe it's time we stopped being so hard on ourselves and others.

PRACTICAL CHANGE

"Sometimes all you need is 20 seconds of insane courage and something great will come of it."

~ Benjamin Mee,
We Bought A Zoo

***Special thanks to Sara Beth Bettis for this one

YOU ARE UNBREAKABLE

Webster's defines unbreakable as: NOT ABLE TO BE BROKEN

There are times when you will embody the definition of this word more than others, you will wear it like a cape–UNBREAKABLE and the people that try to screw with you will quickly come to understand that this word... it is your SUPERPOWER. Weak people allow circumstances to dictate what happens to them, WARRIORS move the circumstances around to suit their needs. Sometimes that is hellish, to walk through heartbreaking betrayal, disappointment, unexpected changes... we fall for a moment, we cry, we are shocked, hurt, stunned, saddened and then we RISE, we change our thinking, we get some gratitude for closed doors, we remember that ALL THINGS WORK TOGETHER FOR GOOD—NO MATTER WHAT KIND OF SHIT STORM IT LOOKS LIKE.

We get up, we get moving, we keep in forward motion, we remember WHO we are. We remember what we have already walked through and we remember that we may bend, however—we DO NOT BREAK— EVER.

We are a special breed, the unbreakables... we understand what 'ripped your heart out' means... we know what 'betrayal' feels like... yet we remain happy and optimistic because we KNOW that we are here to bring LIGHT, to foster GOOD, here to remind people of their strengths... to remind them that they too will RISE.

PRACTICAL CHANGE

"It's one of
the greatest gifts
you can
give yourself,
to forgive.
Forgive everybody."

~ Maya Angelou

USE THE POWER OF FORGIVENESS

The Webster's definition of forgive is to give up resentment against or the desire to punish; to stop being angry with; to pardon; to give up all claim to punish. My working definition of forgive for this chapter is to simply let go.

There are so many people out in the world that are holding onto so much yucky stuff—bad childhoods, terrible marriages/divorces, abuse of some sort, anger from some past wrong done to them, bad business deals, insults, injuries, etc. Every person holding onto something like this feels very strongly about it and should you try to pry it away from them they get very angry. It is their stuff and they want to keep it right where it is, what they fail to realize is that harboring those yucky feelings is sucking the life right out of them.

I have been actively working with forgiveness for several years now as I was holding onto some resentful feelings from the past. Over the last few years as I continued to move forward in my life it became apparent to me that there was something in the way of my progress. After some soul searching I discovered that I was still holding onto resentments and bad feelings toward people from my past. In my speaking I had forgiven them but in my heart I was still willing them to be different and therefore had not truly let go. I started doing some active work on forgiving these people and as a result a 25 year old impossible relationship was miraculously changed. This turn of events was something I never conceived as possible. The power of forgiveness is truly awe inspiring.

When we forgive (let go of) someone or something it doesn't mean that we are consenting to or forgetting what has transpired, it simply means that we are willing to get rid of the dead energy that the situation or relationship has placed on our lives. Holding onto animosity over someone or something doesn't really teach the other person anything it merely interferes with our own ability to manifest good in our lives. Harboring resentments and wishing ill on other people actually stops our own flow of good and can make us sick. People often hold grudges

🐾 PRACTICAL CHANGE

to "teach" the other person a lesson or to try and hurt the other person as they have been hurt. This kind of thinking only ends up hurting us, as we are the ones that actively carry around the bad energy which can cause us to be depressed, overeat, lose sleep or have anxiety.

The Choice Is Yours

In order to forgive someone we had to first decide to take offense from their words or actions. Whenever they did what they did we had a choice to take offense or to let the incident blow over. The choice in that moment was ours. Most people go along in life doing the best that they possibly can for who they are in the moment and often we get angry because their best is not our idea of what the best should be. We think that we would act very differently if we were them, however, we are not them and we don't really know how it feels to be them. It is very easy to be offended by others when we fail to consider what aspects of their lives effect their actions. It is easier to think about forgiving someone when we begin to really think about what their lives are like and what circumstances may be influencing their actions. Perhaps they don't even mean to hurt us, perhaps they are just going along doing the best that they can and they don't even recognize that their actions or words are hurtful.

How we react to something is always our choice. We can choose to be contributed to, insulted or offended. We can choose to take another's actions personally or we can choose to just let things flow over us. If your best friend doesn't call you back you can choose to be angry and offended and make it mean something about your friendship or you can choose to decide that maybe they are just so self-involved that calling you hasn't even crossed their mind. You decide, the choice is yours. The first choice puts a wedge in your friendship and the second allows you to let it go and go on with your life.

Watch Your Frame of Reference

You are not the same person that you were 5 years ago and neither is anyone else you know. Perhaps you are still relating to some people in your life based on how they were in the past. Your frame of reference for certain people could be based on what you knew of them 5, 10 or 15 years ago. This means that when they show up acting differently, you miss it because your frame of reference for them is ingrained in past perceptions. When we hold things against people they tend to remain forever trapped in our minds the way that they were when the hurt occurred. It may be easier to forgive them if we starting looking at whom they have become instead of who they were way back when. This happens a lot with family members, we tend to view them only as we knew them back in the day, who they are now doesn't even show up for us. We all have things in our pasts that we would do differently, imagine how we would feel if someone only judged us from the way we acted at 20.

It is always a good policy to investigate your frame of reference for the people in your life, perhaps some of them deserve a fresh perspective.

Nobody Wins the Blame Game

Blaming other people for circumstances in your life is never helpful nor will it take you any place you want to go. Nobody can win at the blame game. The only way to win in life is to take responsibility for your own destiny. Stop blaming the past and the people in it for what doesn't work in your life. Start having some new thoughts about the people and situations you need to forgive (let go of). Forgiveness doesn't mean that the hurtful behavior is excused or forgotten, it simply means that you stop allowing those incidents to control your life. Forgiveness can take place after you have experienced the necessary emotions associated with the incident. Once the initial anger, sadness, outrage, disappointment, etc. has been processed there is a space for forgiveness. You may need to express your feelings in a constructive way before you can allow the process of forgiveness (letting go) to take place. It is healthy to experience your emotions; it is not healthy to continue to carry around bad feelings for months and years. Process the events and then let them go.

Look For the Lesson

I am a firm believer in the statement 'everything happens for a reason' and I look at every uncomfortable situation in my life and try to see what it wants to teach me. Sometimes I see the lesson right away and sometimes I just have to trust that it's there and that I will see it eventually. I have learned some of my most valuable lessons from the people and situations that have distressed me the most. When you are open to the possibility of being contributed to by every event in your life the unpleasant events seem to go by faster.

I have also learned that one of the best ways to diffuse an attack is to apologize for something right in the middle of it. For instance, "I'm sorry that you feel I've insulted you", or "I'm sorry that you think I hurt you on purpose". People attack you because they want attention or they are unhappy with themselves. If someone attacks you in conversation and you do not respond or you apologize this will diffuse the situation. A person can only fight with you if you let them. You cannot argue with someone who refuses to be engaged by you.

I have been told that what we don't like about other people represents something that we don't like about ourselves. If this is true the first action would be to forgive ourselves for all the things that we find unacceptable. If we can forgive ourselves successfully then we can move ahead to start forgiving others. Truly, truly everyone is going along doing the best that they can for who they are—maybe it's time we stopped being so hard on ourselves and others.

Start With A List

The investigation into forgiveness can be started with a simple list of the people, places and things that you feel you need to forgive and that need to forgive you. Once you have this information written down you can start to think about how best to proceed with the act of letting go.

Everybody has something or someone to forgive and the act of letting go is very freeing to the self and to humanity as a whole. I encourage you to look at where the power of forgiveness might be useful in your life and I promise you that the results from the acts of forgiveness will be magical.

PRACTICAL CHANGE

"There is power and healing in forgiveness! First, we must forgive ourselves so that we can forgive others."

~ Sedrik Newburn
'Unconditional Forgiveness'

BE COMPLETE IN EVERY MOMENT

A dear friend of mine had an unexpected loss recently... a family member had died unexpectedly in the middle of the night from a heart attack... She called to tell me and I just kept saying over and over "Oh my God" and then I started to cry. My friend said she loved me for that... she has a hard time with emotions and it is difficult for her to ask for help or support... my greatest gift to her has always been to express whatever is there... I have always supported her to be complete in every moment.

I talked with her for a long time and I told her that people would say a lot of different things to her over the next days and weeks... most of it kind but meaningless as the majority of folks can't handle death and they will do whatever they can to avoid it... those are the people that say things like, "she is in a better place now". Those of us that have experienced death and not run away from it will tell her the truth... it is horrible, there is nothing more awful, you will have some very dark days and then the shock will fade some and the tears will come less frequently and you will get up and move through your days... you will laugh again and you will be less sad, however there will not be one day that you don't miss the person you have lost and there will be some days where it seems again unbearable.

In the midst of it all if you are a fully functioning person there will be laughter mixed with your tears, there will be some anger at the loss, some "this isn't fair" conversations in your head, some doubt of God's plan... however those of us that have faith in something bigger than ourselves trust that life has a natural order to it and that things happen as they should even if we don't agree.

Mostly people suffer greatly from a death when they are incomplete with the person that died... when they are still holding a grudge or the last words they had were in anger or they didn't say that "I love you"... or they didn't call enough or visit enough... or take time enough to tell people what a gift they are. Those are the undelivered communications that bring you to your knees when someone leaves in an untimely and

🐾 PRACTICAL CHANGE

unexpected fashion. Undelivered communications are what guilt and remorse are made of, I don't recommend them. I was taught at an early age to be complete in every moment... for some people close to me that means an "I love you" almost every time we speak... I think they tire of that, but I don't care much because I know that if anything out of the ordinary happens I have delivered my message.

Walking my friend through her initial shock jerked me back to when my grandfather died... that is another reason people don't deal well with the news of death because it causes them to momentarily relive whatever loss they have experienced and for some folks that is an unbearable thought. People do strange things with death... which is funny because we are all going to leave this planet one day, one way or another... so it seems like there should be less fear and more acceptance.

People might leave this place, however the people that we love are never, ever gone... they are as alive as we make them. My grandfather's pictures are on my bedroom wall, in my hallway and on my desk... I think of him every day and often I can hear his voice in my head still advising me... and I am confident that he has sent certain people into my life to keep his watch... there are pieces of advice that he gave me that continue to shape my life... so for me he is still very much present.

Granted there are several people that I feel like I couldn't live without, yet I don't live in fear of them dying... life has a way of taking care of us if we let it... however we have to let it, which means a certain amount of trust in the process must be present... for many of us this isn't the case.

You Always Have A Choice

Fear comes from thinking thoughts that scare you... you always have a choice... you can choose to think about things that keep you moving forward or you can choose to think about things that stop you.
I highly encourage you to choose to deliver your undelivered communications—unfinished business is bad mojo especially when people die unexpectedly...

"SUCCESS is the
sum of small efforts
repeated DAY IN and
DAY OUT."

~ Robert Collier

DIRECT YOUR MIND

Imagine for a moment that we lived in a world where people actually understood that the words they speak go forward to create their future. In that world there would be very little complaining or negativity and how peaceful it would be. If you were to ask me what I thought was the most important lesson for you in this book my answer would be for you to fully understand that your words, thoughts, feelings and actions create your future.

What we spend our time thinking about, talking about, listening to, looking at, reading and watching all have great bearing on what is created in our lives. Understanding this gives us great power. If your current circumstances are unsatisfactory it is well within your reach to change them. All you need is a little reconstruction coaching.

If you think it, if you speak it- IT WILL COME TO PASS

Direct Your Thoughts

Start to direct your thoughts to what you want more of instead of spending time thinking about what you don't want more of. Stop complaining about the things that aren't working. You have to acknowledge the things that aren't working so that you can correct them; however, there is no need to complain to everyone about them as this will only create more of whatever the problem is. The first step in this process is to merely become conscious about the words that you are speaking. Are you grateful? Do you constantly complain? Are you always talking about what's wrong? Do you speak ill of others? Do you praise and acknowledge people? Do your words inspire people? Do your words hurt people?

Once you have a clear picture of the kind of talking you are doing you can take actions to alter it. Begin to sprinkle some gratitude into your speaking, talk about what went right for the day, make an effort to see the good in situations and speak about that. You have the ability to direct your life and your future by directing your thoughts. You can change your whole outlook on life by simply changing your speaking.

Fake It Till You Make It

In the beginning, doing linguistic surgery on yourself will be extremely uncomfortable as your thoughts will still be the same old moldy ones from the past and your new words will seem stupid. This is where you fake it till you make it. Feelings follow thought so direct thought — direct feeling. After awhile your new thoughts will turn into new feelings. For instance, you will start to talk about how successful you are and pretty soon you will feel like a success and then the circumstances for you to become a success will materialize.

Remember the movie 'Field of Dreams' when Kevin Costner's character built the baseball field and he just kept saying it would work. Everyone thought he was crazy and he just kept right on saying it would work and it did. Real life is actually like that for those of us that understand Universal Principles. You begin by speaking what you intend and then you start moving into the thoughts, feelings and actions that will bring it into being. Lots of times in the middle of doing this you will appear to others as stupid and they may even feel sorry that you are so committed to what they think is a pipe dream.

Think of all the success stories you have heard, they all started out as an idea that had no background of obviousness. Somebody had the thought and they backed it up with feelings and actions and they brought it into being. So can you.

An excellent way to push yourself into new thought patterns is to do affirmations. Find or write affirmations that talk about how you want your life to be and then spend a few minutes each day reading them. I have been doing affirmations since I was 12 years old and these days I spend 20-30 minutes a day doing them. An affirmation is a statement that affirms what you want to have happen. Such as:

🐾 **PRACTICAL CHANGE**

- I am healthy.
- I am successful.
- I am losing weight everyday
- I am grateful.
- I leave behind old states of mind
- I create a future unlike the past

Saying or reading affirmations is a great way to re-train the mind into thinking things that will move you forward.

A Little Gratitude Goes A Long Way

There are so many things to be grateful for and yet most people demonstrate very little gratitude for anything. Expressing gratitude is the quickest way to bring good into your life as what you praise naturally increases. The very act of gratitude is regenerative to the soul. For those of you that aren't sure what gratitude or being grateful actually mean here are Webster's definitions:

Gratitude: *a feeling of thankful appreciation for favors or benefits received; thankfulness*

Grateful: *feeling or expressing gratitude; thankful; appreciative*

When you find yourself in a bad state of mind start mentally listing the things that you have to be grateful for and yes there is ALWAYS something to be grateful for. Taking the time to think about what you are thankful for instead of thinking about what you are suffering from will allow miracles to occur in your life.

I remind myself to practice gratitude daily by making a list every night of what I am grateful for. You can even be grateful for things in advance to help bring them into being. I keep a gratitude journal in my bedside table and I make myself write something in it every night.

Practice some gratitude and I promise that your acts of thankfulness will return to bless you many times over. It is also a great idea to teach children the skills of being grateful as early as possible given that they are our future.

From the Inside Out

True and long lasting change will occur from the inside out and must begin as an idea. Once you have the idea of changing you begin to put a plan in place and the workable plan includes changes in thought patterns, speaking, surroundings, company that you keep, feelings that you have and behaviors that you practice. The first change occurs inside you as you begin to see yourself in the new way. As you see yourself newly you begin to speak and think differently which will cause you to take different actions. Inner behavior starts to change and as a result outer circumstances will follow suit.

It doesn't work to try and start change from the outside in. If you changed your outer circumstances without reconstructing your state of mind the changes wouldn't stick. You can only alter your life from the inside out as your current circumstances were brought on by your current state of mind. Therefore, if you want to change your current circumstances you must first change your current state of mind. Remember that creation occurs in the unseen (mind) and manifests itself into the seen (reality). In other words, whatever you are creating in your mind with your thoughts and feelings will bring itself into manifestation. If you think you are unworthy and poor you will create that. If you think and feel fat and unhealthy you will create that. If you have the power, why not just create yourself as a success?

REPLACE THE NEGATIVE CHATTER IN YOUR HEAD!

Let's talk about replacing thoughts… you have to REPLACE the negative crap in your head with something constructive!

Your thoughts are far more powerful than you might imagine and they go forward to create your future. What you think about, speak about, talk about and give your attention to WILL become your reality, so you have to be very mindful of what you are focused on.

The thoughts that you hold in mind will produce after their own kind and your thoughts will produce an energy field around you that will end up attracting to you the kinds of things that you are thinking.

Remember that character in Peanuts, Pigpen? He had a dirt cloud that surrounded him wherever he went, crappy thoughts will work like that… they will form a dirty cloud around you and they will begin to attract things that are similar. Negative circumstances are no mystery; they arrive because we have given too much attention to negative thoughts, worry, fear and doubt. We will also attract unfavorable circumstances when we are critical, judgmental, angry and ungrateful… like attracts like… that will always be true. Misery loves company.

Thankfully this same principle of 'like attracts like' will work in your favor when you start thinking more positive things, when you are grateful and when you focus on what's good and what works.

There is no EASY button for changing your thinking or for teaching yourself how to stay focused on what you want more of, it requires discipline and work to stay vigilant about your thinking. However, the results that can be produced by this practice are life-altering… you CAN create the life that you want, you just have to be willing to do the work.

"You just do it.
You force yourself
to get up.
You force yourself
to put one foot before the other,
and God damn it,
you refuse to let it get to you.
You fight. You cry. You curse.
Then you go about
the business of living.
That's how I've done it.
There's no other way."

~ Elizabeth Taylor

***Special thanks to Angelica Jimenez for this one

THE VALUE OF FOUNDATIONS & WISDOM

I have been pondering two words over the past couple days... foundation and wisdom. Webster's New World defines Foundation as 'the base on which something rests'... this leads me to consider how many of us, myself included, live our lives resting on a solid foundation. When you build a structure it has to start with a solid and strong foundation, if it doesn't the structure won't hold up. In order to have a successful life you must also start with a solid and strong foundation, otherwise you will have nothing to ground you when the going gets tough... and there are times when the going will get tough.

What makes a solid and strong foundation? Is it integrity, a belief in God, ethics, treating others as you want to be treated, a forgiving heart, an open mind, perseverance, willpower or a combination of all these and more? I say a combination of the aforementioned and more... a solid and strong foundation comes from a belief that you have power in your own life and that you have the ability to change even the direst of circumstances as long as you can keep your wits about you. If you are a constant reaction in the middle of your life you will be incessantly pinging off the walls and in essence will be powerless to change anything. Change can only come from being able to choose your response to a person or situation and this ability is born from having a strong foundation.

If I come from a place of understanding that my life is based on principle and based upon something more than my own pathetic self-concerns then I am able to hold myself in place when life hits me with something unexpected. I am able to observe what is happening and then wisely choose my reaction. If I come from a place of uncertainty, then when life throws a curve ball I have no choice but to scramble and react, react, react.

As far as my life experience shows being a complete reaction has never solved anything, it usually just brings more trouble.

Seems like it would be prudent for us all to give a little thought to what kind of a foundation we have created for ourselves and then to consider if we wake up every morning resting on that foundation... or do we wake up every morning and base our day on the reactions of the moment?

Wisdom is defined by Webster's as 'the power of judging rightly'... my definition of wisdom is something like 'the conclusions you finally arrive at after life has knocked you around enough'...

Wisdom is something that comes over time and thankfully it is something that keeps expanding as we get older. Wisdom is when it finally dawns on you that when you keep behaving the same way and doing the same things, you will get the same result. The opposite of wisdom is insanity which Albert Einstein defines this way, "the definition of insanity is when you keep doing the same thing over and over again and expecting a different result."

How many times have we followed the same path over and over again expecting to end up at a different place? How many of us mirror that mouse running down the same path and still finding no cheese, yet we keep running with the same anticipation and zeal and then we are distraught when the outcome doesn't change. Funny thing is— we KNOW better... on some level we all know better, yet we let our inner wisdom sit it out while we continue to behave like fools.

Practice wisdom today and clear out behavioral insanity... what will you change today?

PRACTICAL CHANGE

HOW BAD DO YOU WANT IT?

Look at your life and pinpoint for yourself some things that you really, really want. Got them? Good. Now tell me how bad do you want them? Do you want them bad enough to change everything about yourself that stands in the way of you getting them? Do you want them bad enough to give up your behaviors that don't work? Do you want them bad enough to not give up until you get them?

Most people will probably tell you that they want certain things, however, I would bet that they are not willing to do WHATEVER it takes to get them and that is why they still do not possess the things that they want. I would also bet that most people don't even fully understand the concept called 'whatever it takes'—most people quit at the first sign of difficulty. There are some people however that don't quit... the Navy Seals don't quit and truly self aware people don't quit either because they know that quitting only perpetuates the circumstances in their lives that they don't like.

Let's talk about where most people lose it along the trail of getting what you want... you start out with a business or a goal or a relationship and everything looks kind of groovy at the beginning. Then we move along in time and obstacles start to appear... the business doesn't seem like such a good idea, the new relationship looks like a piece of shit, the goal you set out to accomplish looks WAY TOO HARD. So you start to buy into that you didn't want it anyway, you start to think of other things that you can do that would be "easier"—we call this the "grass is greener" syndrome—news flash—the grass is NEVER greener somewhere else... smarten up and learn to cultivate your own grass to make it the green that you want it to be—another news flash—this is HARD WORK... it requires commitment, discipline, purposefulness and doing what you said– NO MATTER WHAT. If you want to win and get the things you want in life then you must go to war with all the things about yourself that don't work.

Going to war with yourself means that you set out to prevail no matter what. This means that you must give up paying attention to your ailments, grievances and complaints. This means that you must only look at what you want... keep focused on the goal, the intention and let go of ANYTHING that is counterproductive to forward motion. This looks like doing what you said no matter what opinion you have about it, it means not giving attention and energy to what isn't working, it means NEVER giving up no matter what it looks like all around you... you keep yourself focused on what you want to achieve and you refuse to be swayed by anything that doesn't get you to where you are going.

This kind of war on your self is not easy, in fact it is very, very difficult and therefore the average person would never even begin to attempt it. The average person gets stopped in life by the first sign of trouble... they hit the first obstacle and they quit.

In Navy Seal training an average starting class of 80 people ends up to be about 20 or so by the time graduation rolls around... the men that want to be Navy Seals NO MATTER WHAT are the ones that graduate. In Seal training they are wet, cold, sleep deprived, physically challenged, mentally challenged and pretty much put through what most people have nightmares about—the BEST part of this... they ASK for it... they WANT to go... they strive to EXCEL... they want to be THE BEST... imagine that? Navy Seal candidates want it so bad that they will do anything to get it. Would you go through that kind of hell to get what you want? Are your goals important enough for you to overcome yourself to achieve them?

Any goal or thing worth having is worth whatever challenge you have to go through to get it... that is the beauty inherent in the system of achievement... when you overcome yourself, when you work hard, when you change yourself to achieve something, then you can REALLY HAVE IT... you can REALLY appreciate it, you can feel deserving of it because you know that you EARNED it and it is yours to keep... be it a relationship or a successful business or a degree... whatever.

If you get something and you didn't work for it the satisfaction of it is very short lived... handouts don't teach us anything... challenging ourselves to be better teaches us a wisdom that can't be learned any other way.

🐾 PRACTICAL CHANGE

SOMETIMES YOU GOTTA 'STAND DOW

There are times in life when it is appropriate to 'Stand Down'. .. Military defines 'Stand Down' as the movement of soldiers in combat to a safe place for rest and recovery. It is also a method used by the Military to correct an issue that has been identified as a problem throughout its ranks.

American Heritage Dictionary defines 'Stand Down' as: to withdraw, to end a state of readiness.

Have you ever fought for something so hard only to have it keep whacking you in the face over and over again with its stubborn refusal to yield to your intention?

There comes a time in a wise person's life when the pain and suffering that they have endured to stand by something has exhausted them to the point of heartbreak... a time when they are disillusioned, disappointed, disheartened and discouraged beyond belief... perhaps a time when this something has caused them to feel that people are inherently flawed...

This would signify the time to 'Stand Down'. 'Stand Down' does not mean to give up, instead it means to detach and quell the emotional reactivity of a situation.

Sometimes things have to become worse before they can improve and actually the seeming appearance of 'worse' is really good at work... in disguise.

When you are sure that you have done all you can in regards to a particular situation it may be the time to 'Stand Down'—you will know in your heart of hearts when you have prayed enough, been angry enough, been disappointed enough, been lied to enough, been played enough, been betrayed enough, cried enough, talked enough, yelled enough and worked hard enough.

One day, suddenly perhaps, you will wake up and feel that it is time to 'Stand Down', time to move away from the attachment of that situation... time to let the other characters see the cost of their behavior... time for you to re-group and remember that there is occasionally more power in 'Standing Down' than there is in continuing to 'Stand Up and Fight'.

Some of the best warriors and most brilliant minds have seen the wisdom in a 'Stand Down'. Even those of us that are strong-willed, control freaks can see the value of an occasional 'Stand Down'. There are times when it is better to withdraw than to compete with things that are beneath you or which threaten to drag you down into the muck and mire.

'Stand Down' does not mean that you are weak or that you lack the courage to keep fighting, it means that you are able to see the point in a situation when it is time for you to pull in and observe. When it is time to stop pushing so hard and just let nature take its course. When you have done all your work in a particular situation you can trust that the overall outcome will be for the good, even if the present circumstances resemble a giant garbage dump.

Refreshed, rested, armed with perspective gained from standing down and stepping back, you can re-enter the battle with new commitment and energy.

Life has a way of teaching people what they need to know... and you can count on people's actions returning to them in kind...

If someone loves, they will be loved. If someone harms, they will be harmed. There is no avoiding the cause and effect laws of the universe, no matter who you think you are.

So take heed and if you are faced with a situation that requires it, 'Stand Down' with style and Grace... then get back into action when the timing is right.

🐾 PRACTICAL CHANGE

"Don't mistake my kindness for weakness, for I am kind to everyone, but when someone is unkind to me, weak is not what you are going to remember about me."

- Al Capone

***Special thanks to Rachel Reynolds Carroll for this one

WHERE THE REAL POWER LIES

The real power comes from owning ALL of the things that you have been and that you are... there is a power that comes from owning that shit and that kind of power cannot be gotten any other way. We all have parts of ourselves that we would rather not 'own', times we did things that we are not proud of, behaviors that we wore for a while when we didn't know any better, actions we took when we didn't see any other way. Some of us will call these things the darker part of our story and we shy away from it, it's the stuff that we try not to call attention to... views of our filthy hearts that we would rather not be seen. We ALL have this stuff, I don't care WHO you are or what you would like me to believe about you... every single person has parts we would rather not claim as our own.

Here's the thing though, OWN THAT SHIT!!! You cannot evolve into your best self until you are willing to own ALL the creepy, shitty things about yourself that you wish nobody else knew. The power comes from being authentic and you can only be authentic if you OWN every, single thing about yourself. So many people are busy trying to get you to 'buy' the version of themselves that they wish to present to you and most of their energy floods out to keeping you from knowing the real them... imagine the freedom in simply owning your truth. Stop running from it, stop trying to hide it, stop blaming other people for it! Just SIMPLY OWN IT, whatever it is about you that you wish weren't true or that you want to hide from the world—-JUST OWN THAT! You CANNOT rise PAST IT if you cannot OWN IT!!!! Whatever that thing is, it is not where you are going, and it is just a part of the story that made you. Your power comes from owning those parts of yourself that you find horrible, those parts are not separate from you and they must be included and forgiven in order to move forward. We ALL have those parts of ourselves and we ALL need to own them and move past them so that we can get to where we are GOING...

The next step to being powerful in your life is learning to stand in the middle of whatever seems to be happening and keep your joy and your cool. I have been studying success and prosperity principles since

I was 12 years old, I have been to every seminar and workshop you can imagine and am probably one of the most self-aware and well-trained people you will ever meet and YET I still have days where circumstances appear and try to stop me cold. The last few days have been like that, things have appeared that have made me want to worry, panic, give in to fear-based thought, pull-in, withdraw… take your pick of any response that is reactive and that is where I have been the last few days. The ticket out of that crap is to STAY FOCUSED ON YOUR INTENTION FOR THE OUTCOME—DO NOT under ANY circumstances judge anything by the way it looks in the moment—EVER!

ALL your power comes from being able to stay with your intended outcome and not buy into what 'seems' to be happening around you in the moment, these 'seeming' setbacks or unwelcome things are merely testing you. Will you crumble at the first sign of adversity??? Or will you DRAW A LINE in the sand and REFUSE to be moved???

When life is throwing you stuff that seems unwelcome or unsettling it is simply a test of your strength and resolve, a test to see if you can be shaken off your position, swayed from your intended outcome because if you can be pushed off that easily then you are not worthy to have what you are wanting. You have to be willing to do WHATEVER IT TAKES to get what you want in life, most people run away weeping at the first sign of things not turning out the way they want.

Seeming adversity is merely being used as a sharpening tool—life wants to see if you can stand the heat, if you can stand strong through the storm and remain joyful in the process. It's time to draw a line in the sand and refuse to be moved. It's time to create the life that you want!

BE WILLING TO DO WHATEVER IT TAKES!!!!

Willing to do whatever it takes' is a concept foreign to many, which explains why most people do not have the results that they want in life. 'Willing to do whatever it takes' means just what it says "whatever it takes"... this may mean staying up all night to get the job done, it may mean making cold calls when you don't feel like it, it may mean helping someone if you aren't in the mood, it may mean getting up at 5am to work on your goals before you start your day. It certainly means making yourself uncomfortable in some way, "whatever it takes" is never easy and it never feels good, however it WILL enable you to execute the results you seek.

Sadly, most people that think they work so hard are actually working within their comfort zone, and then they wonder why their HUGE, AUDACIOUS goals never come to pass. Working within your comfort zone will net you the same circumstances and results that you have always had. If things are not moving along the way you want them to, then you are not doing enough to create momentum. Momentum is difficult to create, yet once it starts rolling it will knock down everything in its path and you can keep it moving with consistent focused effort.

If you have a goal that you want to complete then you must be willing to do whatever it takes to make that happen. Do not let anyone deter you, delay you or distract you... keep your head down and stay focused on doing whatever needs to be done. Executing results is not impossible, it simply requires consistency, commitment and a willingness to do 'whatever it takes'. That means no more excuses, only results.

This will be an unpopular way to behave in most circles because the majority of people prefer to offer reasons and excuses instead of results, so if you are truly committed to doing something different you may need to change the company you keep.

IT DOES NOT MATTER HOW YOU "FEEL"

Raising a teenager is an interesting exercise and raising one as a single mom without the Dad involved is sooooo much more interesting… a discussion a moment ago:

Me: Do your oral presentation, you need to video it and review everything before you do.

Boy: That's soooooooooo much work, I don't feel like it, it's too hard.

Me: I don't give a flying xxx how you feel, get up and get moving on it.

Me: NOW WHAT ARE YOU DOING????

Boy: Looking for an apartment, I can't wait to get out of here.

Me: I can send you to Grammy and Papa Steve, then you will really see what's it's like to have to work.

Boy: Just let me film this, you will do it wrong if you help me, just go in your office and DO NOT listen to me making this video.

Me: (Leaving the room, laughing to myself)

Me: (from my office) It sounds great!

Boy: STOP LISTENING!!!!!

I share this moment in time with you because it illustrates the point I want to make about how it doesn't matter how you feel when you need to get something done. Effective and successful people pay very little attention to how they 'feel' in the moment and it certainly never stops them from getting anything done.

We are producing results when we are sad, ill, pissed off, worried, happy, tired and sick of everything. Too many people out there right now operate based on how they 'feel' and then they whine and complain about how their lives don't look the way they want.

There is NO easy button, if you want to make something happen, get off your ass and do something about it… don't tell us how you 'feel', it doesn't matter to us because we are BUSY producing results.

If your life isn't what you want –DO SOMETHING ABOUT IT. My son says I am mean:)—yet here is what I know for sure when this kid leaves my house he will be an effective, contributing member of society able to take care of himself, pay his bills and give back in service to others. I don't care if he 'likes' me, I care that he learns how to produce results and serve humanity.

Most of the time I didn't like my Grandfather or my Mother—I thought they were awful and soooo mean... however if it wasn't for their 'meanness' I would likely have given up when life got really hard years back... some days it is still really hard, yet I am up to the task, well-trained in how to be a warrior... I can thank my 'mean' Italian relatives for that! Thank GOD they had the courage to be 'mean' and that they didn't accept weakness or excuses or whining... because now I am successful in spite of tons of things that tried hard to get in my way.

You can do WHATEVER you set your mind too, you just have to keep pushing through the crap no matter how you feel in the moment. Just keep moving, after a while the obstacles give up and fade away...

FAITH is taking
the first step even
when you can't see
the whole staircase."

~ Martin Luther King Jr.

CALL OUT THE GOOD BY FAITH

Faith is also believing in things not yet seen... this is true even in the most horrid of circumstances, in the midst of those types of circumstances your FAITH will enable you to hold to the fact that there IS GOOD in there somewhere and that the sooner you start calling it out in FAITH, the faster it will APPEAR.

This is a very advanced skill, the being able to call to good in the darkest situation... most people panic, cry, react and run at the first sign of a dark situation... they become immobile in their fear and panic and thereby put themselves at the mercy of the chaos. This is the biggest error that you can ever make, the buying into what something looks like at first glance or first report... this goes for every area of life... work, medical issues, prosperity, and relationship... all of it. Life is designed to TRAIN US to become more skilled and to elevate our soul growth, running around in fear and panic, reacting to things is a very low form of living.

Living that way means that we are at the mercy of whatever crazy circumstance life or the dark wants to throw at us and we have very little stability of Spirit that way because we are only as stable as what things look like in any given moment. So we are like ping pong balls bouncing off the circumstances...

FAITH is trusting that GOOD is in everything, trusting that so much that you get to the point where NOTHING can MOVE you off your foundation... you don't go to the high-high when things look amazing and you don't sink to the low-low when things look like shit...

Calling out the good by FAITH is a skill that will get stronger the more you practice it and you need to practice it... trust that GOD never sets anything up to harm you, therefore no matter what it looks like there is a blessing that can come from it... so start calling to the blessing, trusting that it will reveal itself... and it WILL. Remember that whatever you call a thing it becomes... call it devastating and it will be... call it a BLESSING and it will become that...

PRACTICAL CHANGE

CONTROL YOUR THOUGHTS
(I cannot stress this point enough!!!)

Often we find ourselves 'stuck' in circumstances that we consider unfavorable and we lament them in our thoughts, thinking things like "why me???", "poor me!", "how can this be my life???" etc

We invite these pitiful thoughts in for tea and scones and then invite them back for lunch and dinner. We feel trapped in the circumstances because we keep the thoughts of them alive in our minds. In order to overcome circumstances we MUST learn to overcome ourselves which means manage our thoughts!

When sad, pitiful, failure breeding thoughts step in we have to slam the door on them, we cannot allow them access even for a moment. All it takes is a second and your whole day can be thrown off track by one pathetic thought such as "why don't I have more money?".

You have to be VIGILANT in policing your thoughts. Think ONLY the things that are going to push you forward, STOP entertaining thoughts that make you feel worse!

This morning I was speaking to one of my oldest and dearest friends, he is an amazing man, smart, handsome, talented and witty among other things. He has been in the middle of some trials for the past few years and I fear he is losing heart, this morning I explained to him that at times he is his own worst enemy because he gives voice to the negative chatter in his head. Like so many of us when we are being tried, he feels like it will never end, he feels like this trial has become who he is. That is a FALSE idea; he is a WARRIOR and a CHAMPION as we all are. I know this for him every day and I remind him of it as often as I can. I am reminding YOU as well!

You are an OVERCOMER, A CHAMPION, A WARRIOR! Start ACTING like that; stop suffering by visiting with the negative, stupid, self-defeating chatter in your head.

Only YOU can change the circumstances of your life and you do this by first changing every, single thought you have. If it is an unproductive thought, BANISH it and replace it with something that works... such as 'every day in every way things are getting better and better'—you don't have to know how right now, you just need to know that it IS happening, things are getting better and better...

Action follows thought, control your thinking, be vigilant... and NEVER GIVE IN to that self-defeating crap... NEVER!

"God helps
those who help
themselves."

~ Ben Franklin

ASK GOD FOR HELP...

Even in our darkest hours, help is always available. All we have to do is ASK. Many times we despair over a situation or a circumstance wondering why it is the way it is, and we forget that all we have to do is ask for help. God is ever present, always watching, always listening, and always waiting to provide help—when we ASK.

In order to appreciate the help we receive and to ensure that we will heed Divine Guidance, God waits for us to ask before providing blanket assistance for a situation or circumstance. Asking for help reminds us that we cannot do it alone, it keeps us humble, and it allows us a deep gratitude for what is being given.

Giving things to people when they do not ask can breed resentment. It can also create a feeling of entitlement that causes us to automatically expect that our problems will be solved. Asking allows us to be contributed to, and it allows us to be grateful.

God wants us to remain mindful of the fact that everyone requires help and that no one is too good to ask for it. Some of us love to give help, however, we have a hard time asking for it. It takes a certain amount of wisdom to understand that you can't truly give help if you aren't willing to receive it. You can't be one-sided and live an authentic life... you can't always take and you can't always give. You have to be able to do both things. Some of us have a harder time learning this lesson than others.

We can ask for help from God and we can also ask for help from other people in our lives... everyone can be enriched by asking for help as well as by helping.

Think of something today that you could ask for help with and then go ahead and ask. If you ask for the help it will be provided... go ahead, try it!

"Hey baby,
there ain't
no easy way out!
Hey I'll stand
my ground,
and I won't
back down...
you can stand me
up at the gates of hell
but I won't back down"

~Tom Petty

***Special thanks to Misty Roo for this one

AND THIS IS WHERE I LEAVE YOU...
(for now...)

To wrap up our time together in this particular volume of Practical Change, I am leaving you with some life advice...

• Make sure that you feel 'at home' in your own home. This is your place of grounding and peace, if you can't restore yourself there then everything else will be out of balance

• Keep things in order, houses, desks, closets, cars, papers, etc. Disorder brings disjointed states of mind... it is difficult to operate in excellence with disorder surrounding you

• Get rid of stuff that doesn't serve you—relationships, items, whatever isn't serving you is stealing your energy and holding you back (whether you want to admit it or not)

• Try new things... always

• Don't worry so much about whether or not you are doing things 'right'—life is a process... make adjustments as you go

• Be smart, read, learn... never stop learning

• Be funny and don't be mean

• Don't complain, criticize or make fun of... you get what you give

• Put away money for a rainy day

• Have FUN with your life, we only do this here once, make the most of it

• Cultivate your "REAL" friends, let the superficial bullshit go— it just wastes time

- Enjoy your own company

- LIVE—stop waiting for your 'real' life to begin, these moments right NOW—these ARE your life—so LIVE them OUT LOUD

- Feel your feelings and express them responsibly

- Respond, don't react

- Remember your words have power, use them to help not hurt

- Tell the TRUTH—always—NO EXCEPTIONS

- See yourself as others see you and be mindful of how you treat people and remember karma never loses an address

- Be READY for whatever comes, always have a plan B, maybe C and D too

- Expect the BEST, you deserve that

- Remember that nothing is too good to be true, if you do the work you deserve the reward because you EARNED it

- Don't enable people, let them learn like you have

- Keep your peace—no HIGH highs, no LOW lows—leaders are STABLE people, they keep their JOY in all things and they keep going

- Keep moving forward, don't look back—you are not going that way

- Be aware of your blind spots, we all have them. Work on them and don't let them trip you up—pay attention

- Don't ignore the obvious just because you don't like it, if it is being revealed to you then there is a reason—something there for you to see

- If you have children PARENT THEM, discipline them, teach them to produce results, teach them that actions have consequences. Kids don't need you to be their friends—they need you to be their PARENTS—you are putting people out into the world, so make sure that they are ready.

- Be of service, help others.

- Leave things better than you found them

- If someone shows you a behavior, BELIEVE IT! Actions will tell you everything you need to know about someone. Words are just lip service.

- Don't overthink. When in doubt, go with your gut. Period.

- If it doesn't feel right to you, it ISN'T—-so don't do it. Period.

- TRUST yourself.

- LOVE yourself

- Make peace with your past

- Forgive, not for them, for YOU

- Welcome your future

- Do your best

- And above all—TRUST GOD—ALWAYS—NO EXCEPTIONS!

PRACTICAL CHANGE

"When the
past calls,
let it go to
voicemail.
It has nothing
new to say."

~ Mandy Hale

***Special thanks to Peggy Wittstock for this one

ABOUT THE AUTHOR

Noelle Federico is the owner of Fortunato Partners, Inc., a boutique consulting firm. She is also the driving force behind The Working Single Mom brand. She writes, teaches, speaks and coaches. After 14 plus years, she recently stepped down from her position as CFO, CMO and Business Manager of Dreamstime.com LLC, where she was a member of the founding team that created the global stock photography leader. Her focus has now returned to helping small business people and individuals to succeed

Noelle has over 30 years of experience in all aspects of business management, finance and development as well as media relations, sales and marketing. She teaches Branding and Marketing to small business people and is the author of '**Notes on Branding**' and several other books including '**Practical Change... 8 Ways to Rejuvenate Your Life**'. She is the Founder of the non-profit A Generous Heart, Inc. (www.agenerousheart.com)

Noelle graduated from Fisher College in Boston, MA and also attended Suffolk University. Additionally, she is a graduate of the Dale Carnegie Training.

She lives with her 'soon to graduate' teenage son, Antonio, two large cats and one smaller cat.

You can contact Noelle here, she would love to hear from you...

Noelle@fortunatopartners.com

Connect with her here:

https://www.facebook.com/thewrkingsinglemom/
https://twitter.com/wrkingsinglemom
https://www.instagram.com/wrkingsinglemom/
https://www.linkedin.com/in/noelle-federico/

Or Visit her here:

www.fortunatopartners.com
www.theworkingsinglemom.com

Other Books by One11 Publishing:

PRACTICAL CHANGE

Made in the USA
Middletown, DE
25 August 2021

46912421R00056